Last minute Revision for Data Science

Table of contents:

| Topics Covered |
| Quick Revision |
| Codes Snippets |

Quick revision:

Let's break down the key algorithms and concepts for various areas in machine learning, natural language processing (NLP), computer vision, and related fields. I'll cover the fundamental principles, algorithms, and Python code structures for each topic, followed by important terms and concepts.

1. Machine Learning (ML)

Fundamentals:

- **Supervised Learning:** Training on labeled data to make predictions or classifications.
- **Unsupervised Learning:** Identifying patterns or structures in unlabeled data.
- **Reinforcement Learning:** Learning through interactions and rewards.

Key Algorithms:

- **Linear Regression:** Predicts a continuous value.
- **Logistic Regression:** Classifies data into categories.
- **Decision Trees:** Models decisions with tree-like structures.
- **Random Forests:** Ensemble method using multiple decision trees.
- **Support Vector Machines (SVM):** Finds the optimal hyperplane for classification.
- **K-Means Clustering:** Groups data into clusters based on similarity.
- **Principal Component Analysis (PCA):** Reduces dimensionality by transforming data into principal components.

Python Code Example:

```python
from sklearn.linear_model import LinearRegression
from sklearn.model_selection import train_test_split
from sklearn.metrics import mean_squared_error

# Sample data
X = [[1], [2], [3], [4], [5]]
y = [2, 4, 6, 8, 10]

# Split data
X_train, X_test, y_train, y_test = train_test_split(X, y, test_size=0.2, random_state=0)

# Train model
model = LinearRegression()
model.fit(X_train, y_train)

# Predict
y_pred = model.predict(X_test)

# Evaluate
mse = mean_squared_error(y_test, y_pred)
print('Mean Squared Error:', mse)
```

2. Natural Language Processing (NLP)

Fundamentals:

- **Tokenization:** Splitting text into words or sentences.
- **Part-of-Speech Tagging:** Identifying grammatical parts of speech.
- **Named Entity Recognition (NER):** Identifying entities like names, dates, and locations.
- **Sentiment Analysis:** Determining the sentiment or emotion expressed in text.

Key Algorithms:

- **Bag of Words (BoW):** Represents text as a collection of words.
- **Term Frequency-Inverse Document Frequency (TF-IDF):** Evaluates the importance of a word in a document relative to a collection of documents.
- **Word2Vec:** Converts words into vector representations.
- **Transformers:** Advanced models for handling sequences (e.g., BERT, GPT).

Python Code Example:

```python
from sklearn.feature_extraction.text import TfidfVectorizer

# Sample text data
texts = ["I love programming", "Python is great for machine learning"]
```

```python
# Initialize TF-IDF Vectorizer
vectorizer = TfidfVectorizer()

# Transform texts into TF-IDF features
X = vectorizer.fit_transform(texts)

# Display feature names and their TF-IDF scores
feature_names = vectorizer.get_feature_names_out()
print('Feature Names:', feature_names)
print('TF-IDF Matrix:\n', X.toarray())
```

3. Computer Vision

Fundamentals:

- **Image Classification:** Assigning a label to an image.
- **Object Detection:** Identifying objects within an image.
- **Image Segmentation:** Dividing an image into segments or regions.

Key Algorithms:

- **Convolutional Neural Networks (CNNs):** Specialized neural networks for processing grid-like data (images).
- **Histogram of Oriented Gradients (HOG):** Extracts features for object detection.

Python Code Example (Using CNNs with Keras):

python

Code

```python
from keras.models import Sequential
from keras.layers import Conv2D, MaxPooling2D, Flatten, Dense
from keras.preprocessing.image import ImageDataGenerator

# Initialize the CNN model
model = Sequential([
    Conv2D(32, (3, 3), activation='relu', input_shape=(64, 64, 3)),
    MaxPooling2D(pool_size=(2, 2)),
    Flatten(),
    Dense(128, activation='relu'),
    Dense(1, activation='sigmoid')
])

model.compile(optimizer='adam', loss='binary_crossentropy', metrics=['accuracy'])

# Load and preprocess image data
train_datagen = ImageDataGenerator(rescale=1./255)
train_generator = train_datagen.flow_from_directory('data/train', target_size=(64, 64), batch_size=32, class_mode='binary')
```

```python
# Train the model
model.fit(train_generator, epochs=10)
```

4. Neural Networks

Fundamentals:

- **Neurons:** Basic units that receive inputs, process them, and pass outputs.
- **Layers:** Collections of neurons. Common types include input, hidden, and output layers.
- **Activation Functions:** Functions that introduce non-linearity (e.g., ReLU, Sigmoid).

Key Types:

- **Artificial Neural Networks (ANNs):** Basic neural networks with multiple layers.
- **Deep Neural Networks (DNNs):** ANNs with many hidden layers.

Python Code Example (Using Keras):

```python
Code
from keras.models import Sequential
from keras.layers import Dense

# Initialize the ANN model
model = Sequential([
```

```python
    Dense(64, activation='relu', input_shape=(10,)),
    Dense(32, activation='relu'),
    Dense(1, activation='sigmoid')
])

model.compile(optimizer='adam', loss='binary_crossentropy', metrics=['accuracy'])

# Train and evaluate the model
# X_train and y_train should be defined
model.fit(X_train, y_train, epochs=10)
```

5. Deep Learning

Fundamentals:

- **Deep Learning:** A subset of machine learning involving neural networks with many layers.
- **Backpropagation:** Technique for training neural networks by minimizing the error through the network.

Key Techniques:

- **Convolutional Neural Networks (CNNs):** For image processing.
- **Recurrent Neural Networks (RNNs):** For sequence data.

Python Code Example (Using LSTM for Sequential Data):

python

Code

```python
from keras.models import Sequential
from keras.layers import LSTM, Dense

# Initialize the RNN model
model = Sequential([
    LSTM(50, activation='relu', input_shape=(10, 1)),
    Dense(1)
])

model.compile(optimizer='adam', loss='mean_squared_error')

# Train and evaluate the model
# X_train and y_train should be defined
model.fit(X_train, y_train, epochs=10)
```

6. Generative Adversarial Networks (GANs)

Fundamentals:

- **GANs:** Consist of two networks, a generator and a discriminator, which compete against each other.
- **Generator:** Creates fake data to mimic real data.
- **Discriminator:** Evaluates data to distinguish between real and fake data.

Python Code Example (Using Keras):

```python
Code
from keras.models import Sequential
from keras.layers import Dense, LeakyReLU, BatchNormalization

# Define the generator
generator = Sequential([
    Dense(128, input_dim=100),
    LeakyReLU(alpha=0.2),
    BatchNormalization(),
    Dense(784, activation='tanh')
])

# Define the discriminator
discriminator = Sequential([
    Dense(128, input_dim=784),
    LeakyReLU(alpha=0.2),
    Dense(1, activation='sigmoid')
])

# Define the GAN
gan = Sequential([generator, discriminator])
```

```
# Compile models
discriminator.compile(optimizer='adam', loss='binary_crossentropy')
discriminator.trainable = False
gan.compile(optimizer='adam', loss='binary_crossentropy')
```

7. Transformers

Fundamentals:

- **Transformers:** Models that rely on self-attention mechanisms to handle sequences of data.
- **Attention Mechanism:** Weighs the importance of different parts of the input sequence.

Key Models:

- **BERT (Bidirectional Encoder Representations from Transformers):** For understanding the context of words in a sentence.
- **GPT (Generative Pre-trained Transformer):** For generating human-like text.

Python Code Example (Using Hugging Face Transformers):

python

Code

```
from transformers import pipeline

# Initialize the pipeline for sentiment analysis
```

```python
nlp = pipeline('sentiment-analysis')

# Analyze sentiment
result = nlp("I love using Transformers for NLP tasks!")
print(result)
```

8. Knowledge Graphs

Fundamentals:

- **Knowledge Graphs:** Represent information as entities and relationships between them.
- **Nodes:** Represent entities.
- **Edges:** Represent relationships between entities.

Python Code Example (Using NetworkX for Basic Graph Operations):

python

Code

```python
import networkx as nx

# Create a graph
G = nx.Graph()

# Add nodes and edges
G.add_node('Python')
G.add_node('Machine Learning')
```

G.add_edge('Python', 'Machine Learning')

Display graph information

print(nx.info(G))

9. Artificial Neural Networks (ANNs)

Fundamentals:

- **ANNs:** Networks of interconnected neurons with one or more hidden layers.
- **Feedforward Network:** Information moves in one direction, from input to output.

Python Code Example:

```python
Code
from keras.models import Sequential
from keras.layers import Dense

# Initialize the ANN model
model = Sequential([
    Dense(32, activation='relu', input_shape=(10,)),
    Dense(16, activation='relu'),
    Dense(1, activation='sigmoid')
])
```

```python
model.compile(optimizer='adam', loss='binary_crossentropy', metrics=['accuracy'])

# Train and evaluate the model
# X_train and y_train should be defined
model.fit(X_train, y_train, epochs=10)
```

10. Convolutional Neural Networks (CNNs)

Fundamentals:

- **CNNs:** Specialized for processing grid-like data, such as images.
- **Convolutional Layers:** Apply filters to extract features.
- **Pooling Layers:** Reduce the dimensionality of feature maps.

Python Code Example:

```python
from keras.models import Sequential
from keras.layers import Conv2D, MaxPooling2D, Flatten, Dense

# Initialize the CNN model
model = Sequential([
    Conv2D(32, (3, 3), activation='relu', input_shape=(64, 64, 3)),
```

```
    MaxPooling2D(pool_size=(2, 2)),
    Flatten(),
    Dense(128, activation='relu'),
    Dense(10, activation='softmax')
])

model.compile(optimizer='adam', loss='categorical_crossentropy', metrics=['accuracy'])

# Train the model
# X_train and y_train should be defined
model.fit(X_train, y_train, epochs=10)
```

11. Recurrent Neural Networks (RNNs)

Fundamentals:

- **RNNs:** Suitable for sequential data, with connections forming a directed cycle.
- **LSTM (Long Short-Term Memory):** A type of RNN that can capture long-term dependencies.

Python Code Example:

python

Code

```
from keras.models import Sequential
from keras.layers import LSTM, Dense
```

```python
# Initialize the RNN model
model = Sequential([
    LSTM(50, activation='relu', input_shape=(10, 1)),
    Dense(1)
])

model.compile(optimizer='adam', loss='mean_squared_error')

# Train and evaluate the model
# X_train and y_train should be defined
model.fit(X_train, y_train, epochs=10)
```

12. Deep Neural Networks (DNNs)

Fundamentals:

- **DNNs:** Neural networks with multiple hidden layers.
- **Activation Functions:** Introduce non-linearity (e.g., ReLU, Sigmoid).

Python Code Example:

python

Code

```python
from keras.models import Sequential
from keras.layers import Dense

# Initialize the DNN model
```

```
model = Sequential([
    Dense(64, activation='relu', input_shape=(10,)),
    Dense(64, activation='relu'),
    Dense(1, activation='sigmoid')
])

model.compile(optimizer='adam', loss='binary_crossentropy', metrics=['accuracy'])

# Train and evaluate the model
# X_train and y_train should be defined
model.fit(X_train, y_train, epochs=10)
```

13. Chatbots (Bots)

Fundamentals:

- **Chatbots:** Software applications that simulate human conversation.
- **Rule-Based:** Follow pre-defined rules and scripts.
- **AI-Based:** Use machine learning to understand and respond to user inputs.

Python Code Example (Using NLTK for Basic Rule-Based Chatbot):

python

Code

```
import nltk
```

```
from nltk.chat.util import Chat, reflections

pairs = [
    (r'Hi|Hello', ['Hello! How can I help you today?']),
    (r'What is your name?', ['I am a chatbot created to assist you.']),
    (r'(.*) help (.*)', ['Sure, I am here to help you.'])
]

chatbot = Chat(pairs, reflections)
chatbot.converse()
```

Important Terms List

1. **Algorithm:** A step-by-step procedure for calculations or problem-solving.
2. **Model:** A mathematical representation of a real-world process.
3. **Training:** The process of fitting a model to data.
4. **Validation:** Assessing the model's performance on unseen data during training.
5. **Testing:** Evaluating the model's performance on a separate dataset.
6. **Hyperparameter:** Parameters that are set before the learning process begins.
7. **Feature:** An individual measurable property or characteristic of a phenomenon.

8. **Label:** The output or target variable the model is trying to predict.

9. **Loss Function:** A function that measures how well the model is performing.

10. **Optimizer:** An algorithm to minimize the loss function.

11. **Overfitting:** When a model performs well on training data but poorly on unseen data.

12. **Underfitting:** When a model is too simple to capture the underlying patterns in the data.

13. **Epoch:** One complete pass through the entire training dataset.

These snippets and explanations cover foundational algorithms and concepts across various fields of AI and ML. Each section is designed to be a modular piece of a broader understanding, allowing you to grasp the fundamentals and explore advanced topics.

1. Machine Learning Workflow

Architecture:
- **Data Collection**
- **Data Preprocessing**
- **Feature Selection**
- **Model Training**
- **Evaluation**
- **Prediction**

Diagram:

Explanation:

1. **Data Collection:** Gathering raw data.

2. **Data Preprocessing:** Cleaning and preparing the data (handling missing values, scaling, etc.).

3. **Feature Selection:** Choosing relevant features.

4. **Model Training:** Training the selected machine learning model on the preprocessed data.

5. **Evaluation:** Assessing the model's performance using metrics (e.g., accuracy, F1-score).

6. **Prediction:** Using the trained model to make predictions on new data.

2. Natural Language Processing (NLP) Workflow

Architecture:

- **Text Data Input**
- **Tokenization**
- **Feature Extraction (TF-IDF, Word2Vec)**
- **Model Training (e.g., Classifier)**
- **Prediction**
- **Output Analysis**

Diagram:

Explanation:

1. **Text Data Input:** Raw textual data.

2. **Tokenization:** Splitting text into words or sentences.

3. **Feature Extraction:** Converting text into numerical features (e.g., TF-IDF, Word2Vec).

4. **Model Training:** Training a model on the extracted features.

5. **Prediction:** Making predictions or classifications.

6. **Output Analysis:** Analyzing the results and extracting insights.

3. Computer Vision Workflow

Architecture:

- **Image Data Input**
- **Preprocessing (Resizing, Normalization)**
- **Feature Extraction (CNN Layers)**
- **Model Training**
- **Prediction**
- **Post-Processing (e.g., Bounding Boxes)**

Diagram:

Explanation:

1. **Image Data Input:** Raw image data.
2. **Preprocessing:** Resizing and normalizing images for consistency.
3. **Feature Extraction:** Using CNN layers to extract features from images.
4. **Model Training:** Training the model on the extracted features.
5. **Prediction:** Making predictions on new images.

6. **Post-Processing:** Applying any necessary post-processing steps (e.g., drawing bounding boxes around detected objects).

4. Neural Network Architecture

Architecture:

- **Input Layer**
- **Hidden Layers (Dense, Convolutional, etc.)**
- **Output Layer**

Diagram:

Explanation:

1. **Input Layer:** Receives the raw input data.
2. **Hidden Layers:** Intermediate layers where processing happens (e.g., Dense, Convolutional layers).
3. **Output Layer:** Produces the final prediction or output.

5. Deep Learning Architecture

Architecture:

- **Input Layer**
- **Multiple Hidden Layers (Dense, Convolutional, Recurrent)**
- **Output Layer**

Diagram:

Explanation:

1. **Input Layer:** Accepts the input data.

2. **Multiple Hidden Layers:** Includes various types of layers such as dense, convolutional, or recurrent, each adding complexity.
3. **Output Layer:** Produces the output based on the learned patterns.

6. Generative Adversarial Networks (GANs) Architecture

Architecture:

- **Generator Network**
- **Discriminator Network**
- **Adversarial Training**

Diagram:

Explanation:

1. **Generator Network:** Creates fake data to mimic real data.
2. **Discriminator Network:** Evaluates the data to distinguish between real and fake.
3. **Adversarial Training:** The generator and discriminator are trained together, competing against each other.

7. Transformer Model Architecture

Architecture:

- **Input Embedding**
- **Positional Encoding**
- **Encoder Layers (Self-Attention, Feedforward)**
- **Decoder Layers (Self-Attention, Feedforward)**

- **Output**

Diagram:

Explanation:

1. **Input Embedding:** Converts input tokens into embeddings.
2. **Positional Encoding:** Adds positional information to the embeddings.
3. **Encoder Layers:** Processes input with self-attention and feedforward layers.
4. **Decoder Layers:** Generates output sequences using self-attention and feedforward layers.
5. **Output:** Produces the final output sequence.

8. Knowledge Graph Architecture

Architecture:

- **Nodes (Entities)**
- **Edges (Relationships)**
- **Graph Traversal and Querying**

Diagram:

Explanation:

1. **Nodes:** Represent entities or concepts.
2. **Edges:** Represent relationships between entities.
3. **Graph Traversal and Querying:** Navigating and querying the graph to extract information.

9. Artificial Neural Network (ANN) Architecture

Architecture:
- **Input Layer**
- **Hidden Layers (Fully Connected)**
- **Output Layer**

Diagram:

Explanation:

1. **Input Layer:** Receives input features.
2. **Hidden Layers:** Multiple layers of neurons where processing and learning occur.
3. **Output Layer:** Produces the final output.

10. Convolutional Neural Network (CNN) Architecture

Architecture:
- **Input Layer**
- **Convolutional Layers**
- **Pooling Layers**
- **Fully Connected Layers**
- **Output Layer**

Diagram:

Explanation:

1. **Input Layer:** Receives image data.
2. **Convolutional Layers:** Apply filters to extract features.
3. **Pooling Layers:** Reduce dimensionality and retain important features.

4. **Fully Connected Layers:** Aggregate features and make predictions.
5. **Output Layer:** Produces the final classification or prediction.

11. Recurrent Neural Network (RNN) Architecture

Architecture:

- **Input Layer**
- **Recurrent Layers (e.g., LSTM, GRU)**
- **Output Layer**

Diagram:

Explanation:

1. **Input Layer:** Receives sequential data.
2. **Recurrent Layers:** Handle sequences and maintain temporal information.
3. **Output Layer:** Produces predictions or classifications based on the sequence.

12. Deep Neural Network (DNN) Architecture

Architecture:

- **Input Layer**
- **Multiple Hidden Layers**
- **Output Layer**

Diagram:

Explanation:

1. **Input Layer:** Receives input features.

2. **Multiple Hidden Layers:** Layers of neurons that process data and learn features.

3. **Output Layer:** Produces the final result or prediction.

13. Chatbot Workflow

Architecture:

- **User Input**
- **Natural Language Understanding (NLU)**
- **Dialogue Management**
- **Response Generation**
- **User Output**

Diagram:

Explanation:

1. **User Input:** Text or voice input from the user.

2. **Natural Language Understanding (NLU):** Processes and understands the input.

3. **Dialogue Management:** Determines the appropriate response based on context and user input.

4. **Response Generation:** Generates a response.

5. **User Output:** Delivers the response to the user.

To effectively understand Python code for data science and machine learning, it's useful to break down the libraries into their logical components and see how they fit into the overall workflow. Here's a detailed and logical breakdown for the most common libraries used: **Pandas**, **NumPy**, **Scikit-learn**, **Seaborn**, and **Matplotlib**. This will help you generalize the understanding and see the flow of code more clearly.

1. Pandas

Purpose: Data manipulation and analysis.

Key Components:

- **Data Structures:** Series (1D) and DataFrame (2D).
- **Data Loading:** Read and write data from various formats (CSV, Excel, SQL).
- **Data Cleaning:** Handling missing values, duplicates.
- **Data Manipulation:** Filtering, sorting, grouping.

Logical Flow:

1. **Import Data**
2. **Explore Data**
3. **Clean Data**
4. **Manipulate Data**
5. **Save Data**

Code Example:

python

Code

```
import pandas as pd


# 1. Import Data
df = pd.read_csv('data.csv')  # Load data from a CSV file
```

```python
# 2. Explore Data
print(df.head())        # Display the first few rows
print(df.describe())    # Summary statistics

# 3. Clean Data
df.dropna(inplace=True)    # Drop rows with missing values

# 4. Manipulate Data
df['new_column'] = df['existing_column'] * 2  # Add a new column based on existing data
df_filtered = df[df['column'] > 10]    # Filter data

# 5. Save Data
df.to_csv('cleaned_data.csv', index=False)  # Save the cleaned data to a CSV file
```

2. NumPy

Purpose: Numerical operations and array handling.

Key Components:

- **Arrays:** ndarray for handling multi-dimensional data.
- **Mathematical Functions:** Operations on arrays (e.g., mean, std, dot product).
- **Linear Algebra:** Matrix operations, decompositions.

Logical Flow:

1. **Create Arrays**
2. **Manipulate Arrays**
3. **Perform Mathematical Operations**
4. **Linear Algebra Operations**

Code Example:

python

Code

```python
import numpy as np

# 1. Create Arrays
a = np.array([1, 2, 3])
b = np.array([[1, 2], [3, 4]])

# 2. Manipulate Arrays
a_reshaped = a.reshape(3, 1)  # Reshape array

# 3. Perform Mathematical Operations
sum_a = np.sum(a)          # Sum of elements
mean_b = np.mean(b)        # Mean of elements

# 4. Linear Algebra Operations
dot_product = np.dot(a, a)    # Dot product of arrays
inv_b = np.linalg.inv(b)      # Inverse of matrix
```

3. Scikit-learn

Purpose: Machine learning algorithms and tools.

Key Components:

- **Data Splitting:** Train-test split.
- **Preprocessing:** Scaling, encoding.
- **Model Building:** Training models.
- **Evaluation:** Metrics to evaluate models.

Logical Flow:

1. **Import Data**
2. **Preprocess Data**
3. **Split Data**
4. **Build Model**
5. **Evaluate Model**

Code Example:

python

Code

```
from sklearn.model_selection import train_test_split
from sklearn.preprocessing import StandardScaler
from sklearn.linear_model import LogisticRegression
from sklearn.metrics import accuracy_score


# 1. Import Data
X = df[['feature1', 'feature2']]  # Feature matrix
```

```
y = df['target']           # Target variable


# 2. Preprocess Data
scaler = StandardScaler()
X_scaled = scaler.fit_transform(X)  # Standardize features


# 3. Split Data
X_train, X_test, y_train, y_test = train_test_split(X_scaled, y, test_size=0.2, random_state=42)


# 4. Build Model
model = LogisticRegression()
model.fit(X_train, y_train)        # Train model


# 5. Evaluate Model
y_pred = model.predict(X_test)     # Make predictions
accuracy = accuracy_score(y_test, y_pred)  # Evaluate accuracy
print('Accuracy:', accuracy)
```

4. Seaborn

Purpose: Statistical data visualization.

Key Components:

- **Plot Types:** Histograms, scatter plots, bar plots, etc.

- **Statistical Plots:** Regression plots, pair plots.

Logical Flow:
1. **Import Data**
2. **Create Plots**
3. **Customize Plots**

Code Example:

python

Code

```python
import seaborn as sns
import matplotlib.pyplot as plt

# 1. Import Data
df = pd.read_csv('data.csv')

# 2. Create Plots
sns.histplot(df['column'])  # Histogram of a column
sns.scatterplot(data=df, x='feature1', y='feature2')  # Scatter plot

# 3. Customize Plots
plt.title('Scatter Plot of Feature1 vs Feature2')
plt.xlabel('Feature1')
plt.ylabel('Feature2')
```

plt.show()

5. Matplotlib

Purpose: General-purpose plotting library.

Key Components:
- **Plot Types:** Line plots, bar plots, pie charts.
- **Customizations:** Titles, labels, legends, colors.

Logical Flow:
1. **Create Plot**
2. **Customize Plot**
3. **Save or Show Plot**

Code Example:

python

Code

```
import matplotlib.pyplot as plt

# 1. Create Plot
plt.plot([1, 2, 3], [4, 5, 6], label='Line Plot')

# 2. Customize Plot
plt.title('Line Plot Example')
plt.xlabel('X-axis')
plt.ylabel('Y-axis')
plt.legend()
```

\# 3. Save or Show Plot

plt.savefig('plot.png') # Save plot as image file

plt.show()   # Display plot

General Flow to Understand Code

1. Understand the Purpose: Know what each library is used for (e.g., Pandas for data manipulation, NumPy for numerical operations).

2. Break Down the Code:

- **Identify Inputs and Outputs:** Determine where the data comes from and what the expected results are.
- **Step-by-Step Execution:** Follow the code line by line to see how data is transformed or processed.

3. Libraries Interaction:

- **Pandas and NumPy:** Pandas often uses NumPy for numerical operations under the hood.
- **Scikit-learn and Pandas/NumPy:** Data is typically preprocessed with Pandas/NumPy before being fed into Scikit-learn models.

4. Visualizations:

- **Seaborn and Matplotlib:** Seaborn builds on Matplotlib, so understanding basic Matplotlib commands can help in customizing Seaborn plots.

5. Practice and Experiment:

- **Hands-On Practice:** Write and run code snippets to see how each function and method works.
- **Experiment with Examples:** Modify existing code to understand how changes affect the results.

By breaking down the libraries and their workflows, you can create a clear understanding of how data flows through the system, how transformations are applied, and how results are generated and visualized. This structured approach helps in generalizing the understanding of code and improves your ability to work with different libraries and workflows.

Cleaning data is a crucial step in preparing it for machine learning models. Here's a step-by-step guide to data cleaning, with examples to illustrate each step:

1. Understand Your Data

Objective: Gain an overview of your dataset's structure and contents. **Example:** Load your dataset into a DataFrame (e.g., using Pandas in Python) and use commands like .info(), .describe(), and .head() to get an initial understanding.

python

Code

import pandas as pd

```
df = pd.read_csv('data.csv')
print(df.info())
print(df.describe())
print(df.head())
```

2. Handle Missing Values

Objective: Address missing or null values in your dataset.
Example:

- **Identify Missing Values:**

python

Code

```
print(df.isnull().sum())
```

- **Fill Missing Values:**

python

Code

```
df['column_name'].fillna(df['column_name'].mean(), inplace=True)
```

- **Drop Missing Values:**

python

Code

```
df.dropna(inplace=True)
```

3. Remove Duplicates

Objective: Eliminate duplicate rows to prevent redundant data. **Example:**

python

Code

df.drop_duplicates(inplace=True)

4. Correct Data Types

Objective: Ensure each column has the appropriate data type.
Example:

- **Convert Data Types:**

python

Code

df['date_column'] = pd.to_datetime(df['date_column'])

df['numeric_column'] = df['numeric_column'].astype(float)

5. Normalize Data

Objective: Scale features to a standard range or format.
Example:

- **Normalize Numerical Features:**

python

Code

from sklearn.preprocessing import MinMaxScaler

scaler = MinMaxScaler()

df[['feature1', 'feature2']] = scaler.fit_transform(df[['feature1', 'feature2']])

- **Standardize Numerical Features:**

python

Code

```python
from sklearn.preprocessing import StandardScaler

scaler = StandardScaler()
df[['feature1', 'feature2']] = scaler.fit_transform(df[['feature1', 'feature2']])
```

6. Encode Categorical Variables

Objective: Convert categorical variables into a format suitable for machine learning models. **Example:**

- **One-Hot Encoding:**

python
Code

```python
df = pd.get_dummies(df, columns=['categorical_column'])
```

- **Label Encoding:**

python
Code

```python
from sklearn.preprocessing import LabelEncoder

le = LabelEncoder()
df['categorical_column'] = le.fit_transform(df['categorical_column'])
```

7. Feature Engineering

Objective: Create new features from existing data to improve model performance. **Example:**

- **Extract Date Features:**

python

Code

df['year'] = df['date_column'].dt.year

df['month'] = df['date_column'].dt.month

- **Combine Features:**

python

Code

df['new_feature'] = df['feature1'] * df['feature2']

8. Handle Outliers

Objective: Identify and deal with outliers that may skew the results. **Example:**

- **Visualize Outliers:**

python

Code

import matplotlib.pyplot as plt

plt.boxplot(df['numeric_column'])

plt.show()

- **Remove Outliers:**

python

Code

Q1 = df['numeric_column'].quantile(0.25)

Q3 = df['numeric_column'].quantile(0.75)

IQR = Q3 - Q1

df = df[(df['numeric_column'] >= (Q1 - 1.5 * IQR)) & (df['numeric_column'] <= (Q3 + 1.5 * IQR))]

9. Feature Selection

Objective: Select the most relevant features for your model to improve performance and reduce complexity. **Example:**

- **Using Correlation Matrix:**

python

Code

```
corr = df.corr()
print(corr['target_variable'].sort_values(ascending=False))
```

- **Using Feature Importance from a Model:**

python

Code

```
from sklearn.ensemble import RandomForestClassifier

model = RandomForestClassifier()
model.fit(df.drop('target_variable', axis=1), df['target_variable'])
importance = model.feature_importances_
```

10. Split the Data

Objective: Divide the data into training and testing sets.
Example:

python

Code

from sklearn.model_selection import train_test_split

X = df.drop('target_variable', axis=1)

y = df['target_variable']

X_train, X_test, y_train, y_test = train_test_split(X, y, test_size=0.2, random_state=42)

11. Verify and Validate

Objective: Ensure that the data cleaning steps have been applied correctly and the data is ready for modeling.

Example:

python

Code

print(df.head())

print(df.info())

Summary

Data cleaning involves various steps such as handling missing values, removing duplicates, correcting data types, and encoding categorical variables. Each step prepares the data for better performance and accuracy in machine learning models.

Break down some of the important methods and functions used in data cleaning, focusing on their code structure and usage. I'll explain each method in detail and provide examples for clarity.

1. df.info()

Purpose: Provides a concise summary of the DataFrame, including the number of non-null entries and data types of columns.

Code Structure:

```python
import pandas as pd

# Load dataset
df = pd.read_csv('data.csv')

# Get summary of DataFrame
df.info()
```

Output Includes:
- Number of entries
- Column names
- Non-null counts
- Data types (e.g., int64, float64, object)

2. df.describe()

Purpose: Provides descriptive statistics of numerical columns, including count, mean, standard deviation, min, max, and percentiles.

Code Structure:

```python
import pandas as pd

# Load dataset
df = pd.read_csv('data.csv')

# Get descriptive statistics
df.describe()
```

Output Includes:
- Count
- Mean
- Standard deviation (std)
- Min and max values
- 25th, 50th, and 75th percentiles (quartiles)

3. df.isnull().sum()

Purpose: Identifies missing values in the DataFrame by summing the number of null values per column.

Code Structure:

python

Code

import pandas as pd

Load dataset

df = pd.read_csv('data.csv')

Check for missing values

missing_values = df.isnull().sum()

print(missing_values)

Output Includes:
- Column names and their corresponding count of missing values

4. df.dropna()

Purpose: Removes rows or columns with missing values.

Code Structure:

python

Code

import pandas as pd

Load dataset

df = pd.read_csv('data.csv')

```python
# Drop rows with any missing values
df_cleaned = df.dropna()


# Drop columns with any missing values
df_cleaned = df.dropna(axis=1)
```

Parameters:

- axis=0 (default): Drop rows
- axis=1: Drop columns

5. df.fillna()

Purpose: Fills missing values with a specified value, such as the mean, median, or a constant.

Code Structure:

python

Code

```python
import pandas as pd


# Load dataset
df = pd.read_csv('data.csv')


# Fill missing values with a constant
df_filled = df.fillna(0)


# Fill missing values with the mean of the column
```

df_filled = df.fillna(df.mean())

Parameters:

- value: Scalar, dictionary, or DataFrame to fill missing values

6. df.drop_duplicates()

Purpose: Removes duplicate rows from the DataFrame.

Code Structure:

python

Code

```
import pandas as pd

# Load dataset
df = pd.read_csv('data.csv')

# Drop duplicate rows
df_unique = df.drop_duplicates()
```

Parameters:

- subset: Specify columns to consider for identifying duplicates
- keep: 'first', 'last', or False (drop all duplicates)

7. pd.to_datetime()

Purpose: Converts columns to datetime objects.

Code Structure:

```python
import pandas as pd

# Load dataset
df = pd.read_csv('data.csv')

# Convert column to datetime
df['date_column'] = pd.to_datetime(df['date_column'])
```

Parameters:

- format: Specifies the format of the date string (e.g., '%Y-%m-%d')

8. MinMaxScaler()

Purpose: Scales features to a given range, typically [0, 1].

Code Structure:

```python
from sklearn.preprocessing import MinMaxScaler

# Initialize scaler
scaler = MinMaxScaler()

# Fit and transform data
```

```
scaled_data = scaler.fit_transform(df[['feature1', 'feature2']])
```

Parameters:

- feature_range: Tuple (min, max) for scaling range

9. LabelEncoder()

Purpose: Encodes categorical labels as numeric values.

Code Structure:

python
Code

```python
from sklearn.preprocessing import LabelEncoder

# Initialize encoder
le = LabelEncoder()

# Fit and transform categorical data
df['categorical_column'] = le.fit_transform(df['categorical_column'])
```

Parameters:

- classes_: Array of class labels for the data

10. pd.get_dummies()

Purpose: Converts categorical variables into dummy/indicator variables.

Code Structure:

python

Code

```python
import pandas as pd

# Load dataset
df = pd.read_csv('data.csv')

# Convert categorical column to dummy variables
df_dummies = pd.get_dummies(df, columns=['categorical_column'])
```

Parameters:

- columns: List of columns to encode

11. train_test_split()

Purpose: Splits data into training and testing sets.

Code Structure:

python

Code

```python
from sklearn.model_selection import train_test_split

# Define features and target
X = df.drop('target_variable', axis=1)
y = df['target_variable']

# Split data
```

X_train, X_test, y_train, y_test = train_test_split(X, y, test_size=0.2, random_state=42)

Parameters:

- test_size: Proportion of the data to include in the test split
- random_state: Seed for the random number generator for reproducibility

12. df.corr()

Purpose: Computes the correlation matrix of numerical features.

Code Structure:

python

Code

```python
import pandas as pd

# Load dataset
df = pd.read_csv('data.csv')

# Compute correlation matrix
correlation_matrix = df.corr()
print(correlation_matrix)
```

Output Includes:

- Correlation coefficients between numerical features

13. plt.boxplot()

Purpose: Visualizes data distribution and identifies outliers using boxplots.

Code Structure:

python

Code

```python
import matplotlib.pyplot as plt

# Load dataset
df = pd.read_csv('data.csv')

# Create a boxplot for a numerical column
plt.boxplot(df['numeric_column'])
plt.title('Boxplot of Numeric Column')
plt.show()
```

Output Includes:

- Boxplot showing median, quartiles, and potential outliers

Summary

Understanding these methods is crucial for effective data cleaning and preprocessing. They help in identifying and handling missing values, removing duplicates, scaling features, and preparing the dataset for machine learning models. Each method is designed to address specific aspects of data quality and format, ensuring that the data is in the best possible shape for analysis.

1. Pandas (pd)

Overview: Pandas is a powerful library for data manipulation and analysis. It provides data structures and functions needed to manipulate structured data.

Key Features:

- **DataFrames and Series:** Core data structures for handling tabular data and one-dimensional arrays.

- **Data Loading:** Functions to read data from various formats like CSV, Excel, SQL databases, etc.

- **Data Cleaning:** Methods for handling missing data, filtering, and transforming data.

Commonly Used Functions:

- pd.read_csv(): Reads a CSV file into a DataFrame.
- df.info(): Provides a concise summary of the DataFrame.
- df.describe(): Generates descriptive statistics.
- df.isnull().sum(): Checks for missing values.
- df.dropna(): Drops rows or columns with missing values.
- df.fillna(): Fills missing values with specified values.
- df.drop_duplicates(): Removes duplicate rows.
- df.to_datetime(): Converts a column to datetime format.
- pd.get_dummies(): Converts categorical variables into dummy/indicator variables.
- df.corr(): Computes the correlation matrix.

Example:

python

Code

```
import pandas as pd

# Load dataset
df = pd.read_csv('data.csv')

# Drop duplicates
df = df.drop_duplicates()

# Fill missing values
df = df.fillna(df.mean())

# Convert to datetime
df['date'] = pd.to_datetime(df['date'])
```

2. Scikit-Learn (sklearn)

Overview: Scikit-Learn is a widely used library for machine learning in Python. It provides tools for model building, evaluation, and data preprocessing.

Key Features:

- **Preprocessing:** Methods for scaling, normalizing, encoding categorical features, etc.
- **Model Selection:** Functions for splitting data, tuning models, and cross-validation.

- **Feature Selection:** Techniques for selecting and engineering features.

Commonly Used Modules:

- sklearn.preprocessing: Contains tools for preprocessing data, such as scaling and encoding.
    - **MinMaxScaler**: Scales features to a range.
    - **StandardScaler**: Standardizes features by removing the mean and scaling to unit variance.
    - **LabelEncoder**: Converts categorical labels into numerical format.
- sklearn.model_selection: Contains functions for splitting data and selecting models.
    - **train_test_split**: Splits the dataset into training and testing sets.

Example:

python

Code

```python
from sklearn.preprocessing import MinMaxScaler, LabelEncoder
from sklearn.model_selection import train_test_split

# Initialize scalers
scaler = MinMaxScaler()
le = LabelEncoder()
```

```
# Scale features
df[['feature1', 'feature2']] = scaler.fit_transform(df[['feature1', 'feature2']])

# Encode labels
df['category'] = le.fit_transform(df['category'])

# Split dataset
X = df.drop('target', axis=1)
y = df['target']
X_train, X_test, y_train, y_test = train_test_split(X, y, test_size=0.2, random_state=42)
```

3. Matplotlib (plt)

Overview: Matplotlib is a plotting library for creating static, animated, and interactive visualizations in Python.

Key Features:

- **Customizable Plots:** Supports various types of plots like line, bar, scatter, histogram, etc.
- **Annotations:** Allows adding text, labels, and other annotations to plots.
- **Interactivity:** Provides options for interactive plotting.

Commonly Used Functions:

- plt.boxplot(): Creates a box plot to visualize distributions and outliers.

- plt.hist(): Plots histograms for frequency distributions.
- plt.scatter(): Creates scatter plots for two-dimensional data.

Example:

python

Code

```
import matplotlib.pyplot as plt

# Create a boxplot for a numerical column
plt.boxplot(df['numeric_column'])
plt.title('Boxplot of Numeric Column')
plt.show()
```

4. NumPy (np)

Overview: NumPy is the fundamental package for numerical computing in Python. It supports large, multi-dimensional arrays and matrices, along with a collection of mathematical functions to operate on these arrays.

Key Features:

- **Arrays:** Provides support for high-performance arrays.
- **Mathematical Functions:** Offers a range of mathematical operations for arrays.

Commonly Used Functions:

- np.mean(): Computes the mean of an array.
- np.median(): Computes the median of an array.

- np.std(): Computes the standard deviation of an array.

Example:

python

Code

```
import numpy as np

# Compute mean of a column
mean_value = np.mean(df['numeric_column'])

# Compute median of a column
median_value = np.median(df['numeric_column'])
```

Summary

Each library plays a specific role in data cleaning and preprocessing:

- **Pandas**: Primarily used for data manipulation and analysis.
- **Scikit-Learn**: Provides tools for preprocessing, scaling, and encoding data, as well as for splitting datasets.
- **Matplotlib**: Used for visualizing data distributions and spotting potential outliers.
- **NumPy**: Supports numerical operations and calculations.

By leveraging these libraries, you can efficiently handle various data cleaning tasks, prepare your dataset for machine learning, and gain insights through visualization.

1. CSV Files

Library: pandas

Function: pd.read_csv()

Code Example:

```python
import pandas as pd

# Load CSV file
df = pd.read_csv('data.csv')
```

Tricks and Shortcuts:

- **Specify Delimiter:** For files with different delimiters (e.g., tabs), use the delimiter parameter.

```python
df = pd.read_csv('data.tsv', delimiter='\t')
```

- **Handling Large Files:** Use chunksize to read data in chunks.

```python
chunks = pd.read_csv('large_data.csv', chunksize=10000)
for chunk in chunks:
    process(chunk)
```

- **Specify Columns to Load:** Use usecols to load only specific columns.

python

Code

df = pd.read_csv('data.csv', usecols=['col1', 'col2'])

2. Excel Files

Library: pandas

Function: pd.read_excel()

Code Example:

python

Code

import pandas as pd

Load Excel file

df = pd.read_excel('data.xlsx', sheet_name='Sheet1')

Tricks and Shortcuts:

- **Load Specific Sheet:** Use the sheet_name parameter to specify which sheet to load.

python

Code

df = pd.read_excel('data.xlsx', sheet_name='Sheet2')

- **Load Multiple Sheets:** Use a list of sheet names or None to load all sheets.

python

Code

dfs = pd.read_excel('data.xlsx', sheet_name=['Sheet1', 'Sheet2'])

- **Specify Data Types:** Use the dtype parameter to specify data types for columns.

python

Code

df = pd.read_excel('data.xlsx', dtype={'col1': str})

3. JSON Files

Library: pandas or json

Function: pd.read_json() or json.load()

Code Example:

Using Pandas:

python

Code

```
import pandas as pd

# Load JSON file
df = pd.read_json('data.json')
```

Using json library:

python

Code

```
import json
```

```python
# Load JSON file
with open('data.json', 'r') as file:
    data = json.load(file)
```

Tricks and Shortcuts:

- **Normalize Nested JSON:** Use json_normalize() to flatten nested JSON structures.

python

Code

```python
from pandas import json_normalize

df = json_normalize(data)
```

4. SQL Databases

Library: pandas and sqlalchemy

Function: pd.read_sql()

Code Example:

python

Code

```python
import pandas as pd
from sqlalchemy import create_engine

# Create a SQLAlchemy engine
engine = create_engine('sqlite:///database.db')
```

```
# Load SQL table into DataFrame
df = pd.read_sql('SELECT * FROM table_name', engine)
```

Tricks and Shortcuts:

- **Read SQL Query:** Use raw SQL queries to load specific subsets of data.

python

Code

```
df = pd.read_sql('SELECT column1, column2 FROM table_name WHERE condition', engine)
```

- **Specify Index Column:** Use the index_col parameter to set an index column.

python

Code

```
df = pd.read_sql('SELECT * FROM table_name', engine, index_col='id')
```

5. Parquet Files

Library: pandas and pyarrow or fastparquet

Function: pd.read_parquet()

Code Example:

python

Code

```
import pandas as pd
```

```
# Load Parquet file
df = pd.read_parquet('data.parquet')
```

Tricks and Shortcuts:

- **Read with Specific Engine:** Use engine to specify pyarrow or fastparquet.

python

Code

```
df = pd.read_parquet('data.parquet', engine='pyarrow')
```

6. HDF5 Files

Library: pandas and tables

Function: pd.read_hdf()

Code Example:

python

Code

```
import pandas as pd

# Load HDF5 file
df = pd.read_hdf('data.h5', key='df')
```

Tricks and Shortcuts:

- **Specify Key:** Use the key parameter to specify the HDF5 group or dataset name.

python

Code

df = pd.read_hdf('data.h5', key='my_group/my_dataset')

7. Feather Files

Library: pandas and pyarrow

Function: pd.read_feather()

Code Example:

python

Code

```
import pandas as pd

# Load Feather file
df = pd.read_feather('data.feather')
```

Tricks and Shortcuts:

- **Efficient Storage:** Feather files are optimized for fast reads and writes.

8. SAS Files

Library: pandas and sas7bdat

Function: pd.read_sas()

Code Example:

python

Code

```
import pandas as pd

# Load SAS file
```

```
df = pd.read_sas('data.sas7bdat')
```

Tricks and Shortcuts:

- **Specify Encoding:** Use the encoding parameter if needed.

python

Code

```
df = pd.read_sas('data.sas7bdat', encoding='latin1')
```

9. Google Sheets

Library: gspread and pandas

Function: gspread for reading Google Sheets, pd.DataFrame for converting to DataFrame

Code Example:

python

Code

```
import gspread
import pandas as pd
from oauth2client.service_account import ServiceAccountCredentials

# Authenticate and create a client
scope = ["https://spreadsheets.google.com/feeds", "https://www.googleapis.com/auth/drive"]
```

```
creds = ServiceAccountCredentials.from_json_keyfile_name('credentials.json', scope)

client = gspread.authorize(creds)


# Open the Google Sheet
sheet = client.open('SheetName').sheet1


# Load data into DataFrame
data = sheet.get_all_records()
df = pd.DataFrame(data)
```

Tricks and Shortcuts:

- **Update Credentials:** Ensure your credentials JSON file is up-to-date.
- **Use Batch Requests:** Optimize data retrieval with batch requests if needed.

Summary

Here's a quick reference for common file formats and libraries:

- **CSV:** pandas.read_csv()
- **Excel:** pandas.read_excel()
- **JSON:** pandas.read_json() or json.load()
- **SQL:** pandas.read_sql()
- **Parquet:** pandas.read_parquet()

- **HDF5:** pandas.read_hdf()
- **Feather:** pandas.read_feather()
- **SAS:** pandas.read_sas()
- **Google Sheets:** gspread and pandas

These methods and tricks will help you efficiently load and preprocess data from various sources.

python snippets used in AIML break it down into manageable understanding parts

In the context of Artificial Intelligence (AI) and Machine Learning (ML), Python snippets cover a wide range of tasks, including data manipulation, model training, evaluation, and deployment. Here, I'll break down some essential Python snippets and concepts used in AI and ML, explaining each part for clarity.

1. Loading Data

Snippet:

python

Code

```
import pandas as pd

# Load a CSV file into a DataFrame
df = pd.read_csv('data.csv')
```

```
# Display the first few rows of the DataFrame
print(df.head())
```

Breakdown:

- **import pandas as pd:** Imports the Pandas library, which is used for data manipulation and analysis.
- **pd.read_csv('data.csv'):** Reads data from a CSV file into a DataFrame.
- **df.head():** Displays the first five rows of the DataFrame to give a quick look at the data.

2. Handling Missing Values

Snippet:

python

Code

```
# Fill missing values with the mean of the column
df.fillna(df.mean(), inplace=True)

# Drop rows with any missing values
df.dropna(inplace=True)
```

Breakdown:

- **df.fillna(df.mean(), inplace=True):** Replaces missing values with the mean of each column. inplace=True modifies the DataFrame in place.

- **df.dropna(inplace=True):** Removes rows with missing values.

3. Feature Scaling

Snippet:

python

Code

from sklearn.preprocessing import StandardScaler

# Initialize the scaler
scaler = StandardScaler()

# Fit and transform the data
scaled_features = scaler.fit_transform(df[['feature1', 'feature2']])

Breakdown:

- **from sklearn.preprocessing import StandardScaler:** Imports the StandardScaler class from Scikit-Learn.
- **scaler = StandardScaler():** Initializes the scaler object.
- **scaler.fit_transform(df[['feature1', 'feature2']]):** Fits the scaler on the specified features and scales them.

4. Encoding Categorical Variables

Snippet:

python

Code

```python
from sklearn.preprocessing import OneHotEncoder

# Initialize the encoder
encoder = OneHotEncoder(sparse=False)

# Fit and transform categorical data
encoded_features = encoder.fit_transform(df[['categorical_column']])
```

Breakdown:

- **from sklearn.preprocessing import OneHotEncoder:** Imports the OneHotEncoder class from Scikit-Learn.
- **encoder = OneHotEncoder(sparse=False):** Initializes the encoder with sparse=False to return a dense array.
- **encoder.fit_transform(df[['categorical_column']]):** Encodes the categorical column into one-hot format.

5. Splitting Data into Training and Testing Sets

Snippet:

python

Code

```python
from sklearn.model_selection import train_test_split

# Define features and target
X = df.drop('target', axis=1)
y = df['target']
```

```python
# Split data into training and testing sets
X_train, X_test, y_train, y_test = train_test_split(X, y, test_size=0.2, random_state=42)
```

Breakdown:

- **from sklearn.model_selection import train_test_split:** Imports the train_test_split function.
- **X = df.drop('target', axis=1):** Separates features from the target variable.
- **y = df['target']:** Defines the target variable.
- **train_test_split(X, y, test_size=0.2, random_state=42):** Splits the data into training and testing sets, with 20% of the data reserved for testing.

6. Training a Model

Snippet:

python

Code

```python
from sklearn.ensemble import RandomForestClassifier

# Initialize the model
model = RandomForestClassifier(n_estimators=100, random_state=42)


# Train the model
```

model.fit(X_train, y_train)

Breakdown:

- **from sklearn.ensemble import RandomForestClassifier:** Imports the RandomForestClassifier class.

- **model = RandomForestClassifier(n_estimators=100, random_state=42):** Initializes the RandomForestClassifier with 100 trees.

- **model.fit(X_train, y_train):** Trains the model using the training data.

7. Making Predictions

Snippet:

python

Code

```
# Make predictions on the test set
y_pred = model.predict(X_test)
```

Breakdown:

- **model.predict(X_test):** Uses the trained model to make predictions on the test set.

8. Evaluating the Model

Snippet:

python

Code

from sklearn.metrics import accuracy_score, confusion_matrix

```python
# Calculate accuracy
accuracy = accuracy_score(y_test, y_pred)
print('Accuracy:', accuracy)

# Generate confusion matrix
conf_matrix = confusion_matrix(y_test, y_pred)
print('Confusion Matrix:\n', conf_matrix)
```

Breakdown:

- **from sklearn.metrics import accuracy_score, confusion_matrix:** Imports functions to evaluate the model.
- **accuracy_score(y_test, y_pred):** Calculates the accuracy of the model.
- **confusion_matrix(y_test, y_pred):** Generates a confusion matrix to evaluate classification performance.

9. Saving and Loading a Model

Snippet:

python

Code

```python
import joblib

# Save the model
joblib.dump(model, 'model.pkl')
```

# Load the model
loaded_model = joblib.load('model.pkl')

Breakdown:

- **import joblib:** Imports the joblib library for model serialization.
- **joblib.dump(model, 'model.pkl'):** Saves the model to a file.
- **joblib.load('model.pkl'):** Loads the model from the file.

10. Visualizing Data

Snippet:

python

Code

import matplotlib.pyplot as plt

# Plot a histogram of a feature
plt.hist(df['feature1'])
plt.title('Histogram of Feature 1')
plt.xlabel('Value')
plt.ylabel('Frequency')
plt.show()

Breakdown:

- **import matplotlib.pyplot as plt:** Imports Matplotlib's pyplot for plotting.

- **plt.hist(df['feature1']):** Creates a histogram of the specified feature.
- **plt.show():** Displays the plot.

Summary

Here's a quick reference for the snippets:

1. **Loading Data:** pd.read_csv(), pd.read_excel()
2. **Handling Missing Values:** df.fillna(), df.dropna()
3. **Feature Scaling:** StandardScaler
4. **Encoding Categorical Variables:** OneHotEncoder
5. **Splitting Data:** train_test_split()
6. **Training a Model:** RandomForestClassifier.fit()
7. **Making Predictions:** model.predict()
8. **Evaluating the Model:** accuracy_score(), confusion_matrix()
9. **Saving/Loading a Model:** joblib.dump(), joblib.load()
10. **Visualizing Data:** matplotlib.pyplot

These snippets cover fundamental tasks in AI and ML, from data handling to model evaluation and visualization. Each snippet is modular, allowing you to build a comprehensive workflow for data science projects.

www.ingramcontent.com/pod-product-compliance
Lightning Source LLC
Chambersburg PA
CBHW082238220526
45479CB00005B/1275